UPDATED

THE
MONEY MAP

FINALLY... YOUR SIMPLE ONE PAGE PLAN
FOR RETIREMENT AND INVESTMENT SUCCESS

UPDATED

THE
MONEY MAP

FINALLY... YOUR SIMPLE ONE PAGE PLAN
FOR RETIREMENT AND INVESTMENT SUCCESS

JOEL M. JOHNSON, CFP ®

Printed in the United States of America.

ISBN: 978-1-63385-300-3

Designed and published by

Word Association Publishers
205 Fifth Avenue
Tarentum, Pennsylvania 15084

www.wordassociation.com
1.800.827.7903

TABLE OF CONTENTS

REGULATORY ISSUES: NOTE TO READERS 1

INTRODUCTION TO THE MONEY MAP 3

1. HEY, WHERE ARE YOU GOING?
   CHOOSING A DESTINATION 6

2. TAKING ADVICE FROM BIASED SOURCES. 10

3. STOCK MARKET HISTORY 18

4. GREED - ENTITLEMENT - ARROGANCE
   THE CULTURE OF WALL STREET 28

5. WHO WANTS TO TAKE YOUR MONEY? 35

6. THE TRUTH ABOUT MUTUAL FUNDS. 46

7. WHY REAL ESTATE WORKS 51

8. THE ONE-PAGE ROADMAP FOR YOUR FINANCES 57

9. THE MONEY MAP: YOUR ENTIRE LIFE ON ONE PAGE 64

10. IT'S ALL ABOUT INCOME 71

11. INVESTMENTS DESIGNED TO PRODUCE INCOME. 79

12. THE KNOCKOUT PUNCH TO THE TAXMAN 92

13. HOW TO CHOOSE THE RIGHT FINANCIAL ADVISOR 106

REGULATORY ISSUES
NOTE TO READERS

This publication contains the opinions and ideas of its author. The strategies outlined in this book may not be suitable for every individual and are not guaranteed or warranted to produce any particular results. Presentation of performance data herein does not imply that similar results will be achieved in the future. Any such data is provided merely for illustrative and discussion purposes; rather than focusing on the time periods used or the results derived, the reader should focus instead on the underlying principles.

This book is sold with the understanding that neither publisher nor author, through his book, is engaged in rendering legal, tax, investment, insurance, financial, accounting, or other professional advice or services. If the reader requires such advice or services, a competent professional should be consulted. Relevant laws vary from state to state.

No warranty is made with respect to the accuracy or the completeness of the information contained herein, and both the author and the publisher specifically disclaim any responsibility for any liability, loss, or risk, personal or otherwise, that is incurred as a consequence, directly or indirectly, of the use and application of any of the contents of this book.

INTRODUCTION TO THE MONEY MAP

Over the past 20 years I have personally met with thousands of people-families and individuals, rich and poor, young and old, those who are brilliant and others of average intelligence. I have helped many of these people, but unfortunately some of them decided not to follow the advice they were given. In essence, they were unwilling to be helped. Not all, but some of those folks paid a dear, dear price. I can think of many individuals who lost money or opportunities by not following good advice. Sometimes these losses were due to bad advice other mistakes were based on reactive decisions that came from fear.

There are a number of reasons why individuals and families don't do the right thing when it comes to their money. We're going to explore that in the Money Map, but more important, we're going to explore ways that you can get your financial house in order in a very simple way.

In this book I will share some of the techniques that I have learned over my many years in the investment and retirement planning business. I will also share with you some of the dirty little secrets of Wall Street, some of the things that go on behind the scenes that can hurt your financial security.

I look forward to your exploring these strategies that we put together in this book and possibly bettering your financial future for the benefit of yourself and your family.

A little bit about myself: I, along with my business partners have built a firm that serves thousands of clients in the greater northeastern part of our United States. We do investment planning and insurance planning. We help clients to reduce taxes and to grow wealth. Our primary focus is on helping retirees to protect their nest eggs, to grow their nest eggs, and maybe even more important than that, to keep their savings safe from the people who are trying to take it. Taxes, lawyers, and even our local and state governments are all in line to take our money. Sometimes it's that son or daughter-in-law who is in line to take our money. How do we protect our money? How do we grow our money? How can we plan our retirement to reflect our goals and values in life. The fear for many Americans is that they may run out of money before they die. The job of a good financial planner is to do everything possible to help prevent that from happening.

CHAPTER 1

HEY, WHERE ARE YOU GOING?
GOALS: CHOOSING A DESTINATION

Begin with the end in mind—Steven Covey

Here's a great exercise I have my clients do in the planning process that is very effective and helps visually clarify a destination. I will tell them, "Pretend there were no restrictions or rules, and forget everything you think you know about your financial situation. If you could wave a magic wand and solve your biggest financial concern right now, what would that problem be? Go ahead—on a separate piece of paper write down that problem. Next, write down all the feelings you would have if this one issue was fixed. After that, close your eyes and visualize exactly what the outcome would look like. How would it change your life? How would it change your relationships? Again, how would you feel?"

The most important question I then ask is, "Do you want me to help you fix this problem?"

As an advisor, I can help only if people want me to help, but it's very important that they choose their goals and tell me what their financial concerns are. The problem in this business of giving financial advice is that too many financial advisors go to client meetings with their own agenda. They want to sell an annuity, a mutual fund, or some life insurance policy. They want to sell the latest and greatest scheme that their Wall Street brokerage firm has come up with to make money. That's not about the client, is it?

In our business it *is* about the client, and we simply ask people, "What are your concerns?" And then we help them decide if they are prepared to take action to address those concerns. Can they be fixed? Then we simply ask the client, "Would you like me to help you fix this?" And that is the exact wording I use. "Would you like me to help you fix this?"

So being financially successful takes knowing your destination and understanding why it is important for you to get there. Not just the logical reasons or benefits, but the emotional reasons. One of the most important words I used in this chapter so far is *feelings*. Emotions, not logic, dictate our human behavior. A concern is emotional. A financial concern is emotional. A fear is emotional. The first item on your Money Map should be your biggest concern. When you have identified where you are going, a good advisor can help you get there.

Once you have expressed a goal, it is time to figure out how you can get there. Most financial goals take money. Many times, changes need to be made. Many of the changes we help our clients make involve changing investment strategies. Let's be realistic here. The job of a financial advisor is to coach you into establishing realistic goals, and to help you when the going gets tough.

Sometimes it means going in a direction that is counterintuitive, such as delaying saving for retirement in order to pay down debt. Another counterintuitive decision that I have recommended before is the following: if you have to choose between saving for your retirement and saving for your kids' education, then save for retirement. Look at it this way: your kids can take out student loans or work while in college or both. Believe me, they will be okay, and maybe even better off because of it. However, if you don't save for your retirement, you'll be living with your well-educated kids. Is that what you want? Tough choices have to be made. That is why it is so important to *feel* the benefits of the goal. Only then will you be able to make those tough choices and stick with them.

Remember to begin with the end in mind: literally write your goals down. Be crystal clear. We like our clients to write it down on their Money Maps in their own handwriting, and then our mission is to help them reach these goals. Get a coach, a financial advisor who can help.

One last item to keep in mind: just as successful athletes focus on one game or match at a time, successful investors focus on one issue at a time. They fix it, and then they move on to the next one.

CHAPTER 2

TAKING ADVICE FROM BIASED SOURCES

Many people act on advice from parties they don't even know. Sometimes the advice comes from financial magazines or from somebody on TV, maybe even a book like this one. You need to be very careful of this. As a general rule, do not act on advice from anyone who does not know your individual situation—everyone's finances are unique. What might be great advice for one person might be terrible advice for another. In fact, it may be advice that financially ruins the other person. Think of a doctor's prescription that could save one person's life yet kill another.

The other critical fact we have to understand is that at times advice comes from biased sources, from individuals who have a direct financial interest in your being steered a certain way. It is so important if you're using a financial advisor, which I recommend that you do, that you find somebody you can trust, someone who shares your values.

Let's talk about the relationship with your doctor for a minute. Do you trust your doctor? I feel very good about mine, who has been my doctor for many years. He is about seven miles away from my house, and he knows my situation, I feel comfortable with him. He's caring. He always returns phone calls the same day; I can't think of a time that he has not. So I appreciate my doctor.

Your doctor makes more money if he performs an operation on you than if he simply gives you exercises to do to solve, let's say, a knee injury. Orthopedic surgeons make a lot. But such a surgeon may also recommend just some exercise, maybe swimming or stretching exercises that will solve the problem. You have to trust that if he recommends knee surgery, it is indeed in your best interest—he could be biased and trying just to make extra money. This is what is called a conflict of interest. When someone makes more money by recommending one course of action over another. It is impossible to remove all conflicts of interest in life so it is important to be able to trust the advice-giver.

Now let's talk about some of the biases in the financial services business. First of all, let's consider financial magazines; you can typically find anywhere from five to fifteen financial publications just at your grocery store. *Money Magazine, Forbes, Fortune, Worth,* and various other publications will offer you financial advice. But how do these magazines really make money? Advertising revenues, for the most part; the subscription price really just covers the distribution. Next time you're in a grocery store, pick up one of those magazines and look at the back cover, and then the inside front cover, and then the inside back cover, the most expensive spots to advertise. Then look inside at the full-page ads many times. The biggest advertisers in these magazines are mutual fund firms and Wall Street firms.

These magazines come out with a top-10 list every year. You know what I mean: *Money Magazine* will list this year's top 10 mutual funds or the worst-performing funds. Let's say a mutual fund company such as Franklin Templeton buys the back covers of *Money*

Magazine throughout the year. Do you know how much money that costs? It's a substantial commitment for Franklin Templeton, probably in the multimillions of dollars. Do you think that when *Money Magazine* puts together its worst-funds list in a certain year it is going to be a little biased to make sure that Franklin Templeton doesn't get on that list? Maybe. I don't know. I'm not saying the people at *Money Magazine* are good or bad; I'm just trying to point out a potential bias in the market place.

Let's talk about another bias. Do Wall Street firms make more money selling you risky investments or selling you safe investments? When I say safe, I mean investments that either cannot go down or offer the investor an extremely low probability of losing value—something with some type of a guarantee, preferably a government guarantee. So I ask the question again, do Wall Street firms make more money off of you when your money is safe or at risk? Well, I can tell you that they make the most money when your money is at risk. As a matter of fact, this whole system that they have—beautiful offices around the country and retail brokers who are there to sell things to clients—would not exist if everybody with an account at a big Wall Street firm put his or her money just in CDs and government bonds; there is not enough profit in those products to support that distribution system. They have to have accounts with risk money in it so they can borrow against that money to trade for their own accounts. They also have to have that money at risk so brokers can move it around and generate additional commissions and so they can lend those securities to other parties *who want to bet against your stocks going up*. Sometimes it's even your firm that is betting against your stocks going up.

This creates a dilemma, because for most people the day they retire represents a fundamental change in their lives, and it should also represent a fundamental change in their investment strategy. Many times instead of making a bigger portion of your money safe, they just simply move it around to different mutual funds.

We discuss in another area of this book the difference between bond funds and stock funds and that bond funds are still risky; nonetheless, when you retire, you just get a bigger allocation of bond mutual funds with many brokerage firms.

It is important to understand the biases and remember the value in dealing with independent financial advisors and certified financial planners. I was trained by a Wall Street firm; we would have certain lists of stocks we were supposed to push, stocks that would make the firm the most money. It is my understanding that this still goes on today.

Sometimes there are certain investments that are perfect for a client, but if I work for a certain firm, I cannot necessarily recommend those investments. If I am an employee of a large brokerage firm, I do not have independence.

I'm not saying all large Wall Street brokerage firms are bad. It is just important to be aware of the biases that exist in financial magazines and Wall Street firms, but realize that I am not saying to immediately close your account right now—just be aware of those biases. I am also not saying that everybody who works for a big Wall Street firm is bad. I have friends who work for big Wall Street firms, and some of them have been there most of their careers. Those firms have them so locked up with pension benefits and deferred compensation plans that they can't leave unless they really want to hurt their families financially, so some of them are kind of stuck. You can still find a person at those firms who will act in your best interest, but the pressure on brokers at Wall Street firms is very heavy, and there are certain investments and products that they have to recommend. Nowadays we also see brokerage companies that are owned by banks giving their brokers extra compensation if they sell bank products like mortgages.

INSURANCE COMPANIES

Let's talk about insurance companies. If you go to an insurance company or somebody who is a "financial advisor" who happens to work for a big insurance company such as MassMutual or MetLife or Northwestern Mutual, chances are that their compensation structure is set up so that the advisor makes the most money by selling you insurance, and you have to understand this. Does this mean that your person at such a company is a bad advisor? No, not necessarily, but you have to understand that there is a system in those companies by which they get paid more money to sell insurance products.

Is it important to understand these biases? Yes, it is. Does that mean a person who works for these companies cannot do a good job for you? No; I think some can do a good job for you.

The last area I would like to address is a broker who works for a bank. Yes, there are some good advisors who work at the bank branch, however, you may get a less-experienced advisor.

Having a good and independent financial advisor, in my opinion, is very critical because some of those biases will be removed. Independent financial advisors pay their own bills, and independent financial firms are out on their own to make it in the marketplace. If they are successful, and have been around for a while, they may be serving their clients well.

CHAPTER 3

STOCK MARKET HISTORY

Picture this: You have an investment account that is going down; you see that each time you get your statement. The news about the economy is not good, and you're concerned that your account might continue to decline. You tell your broker that you're worried and maybe you should get out of the investments that are going down. What does the broker say to you? You tend to hear things such as, "Hang in there," "The market always comes back," "You're in it for the long run," and "You haven't lost money until you sell." I say *hogwash*, and I'm being polite with my language here.

Remember, it's your money, not theirs. Although there may be some truth to these statements, the uncertainty you feel at a time like this can suck the joy right out of your retirement.

Let's examine some stock market periods and you judge. Do you want to gamble with your hard-earned retirement money and risk going into one of these periods? Chart 1 shows the Dow Jones Industrial Average from October 1928 to December 1949. Yes, you're reading it correctly. The Dow was at 375 in 1929, and 20 years later it was at 200. Down a total of 47% in 20 years. Now you're saying that that was the Great Depression, an exception. Oh, really? Let's look at Chart 2, the NASDAQ from December 27, 1999, to December 28, 2009. The NASDAQ went from 5,000 to 2,300 in 10 years. It took until May of 2015 to get back to 5,000, meanwhile, the fear and lack of patience caused many people to make bad investment decisions over this 16-year period.

Now, some compare our present-day economy after the real estate and banking crisis to Japan's in 1990 when that country had its real estate crisis. Let's look at Chart 3. In 1990, the Nikkei, the Japanese equivalent of our Dow, was at 35,000. In December 2009, 19 or 20 years later, it was at around 11,000. That's a total loss of 69% in 20 years.

Last, let's look at the Dow from 1964 to 1982. On Chart 4, you'll notice that the Dow over this 18-year period was basically flat. Also notice that there were five one- to two-year periods during which if you could have caught some of the upside of the Dow and not lost money during the following downturns, you probably could have earned a reasonable rate of return during this period as indicated by the lines across the chart.

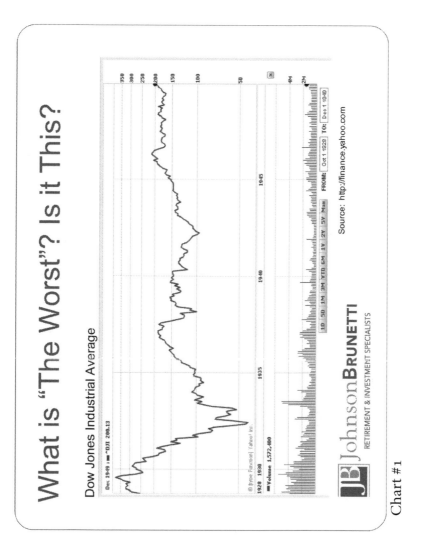

How About This?

Chart #2

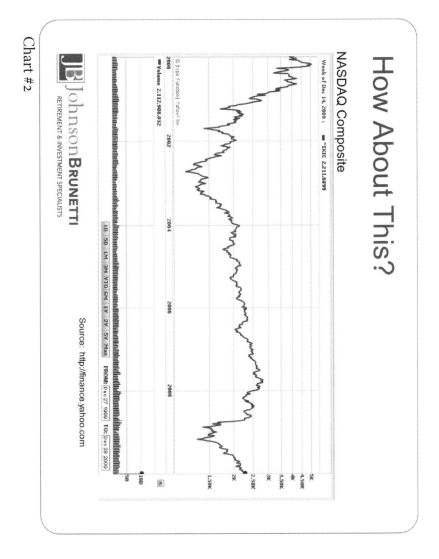

Source: http://finance.yahoo.com

Or Maybe This?

Nikkei 225

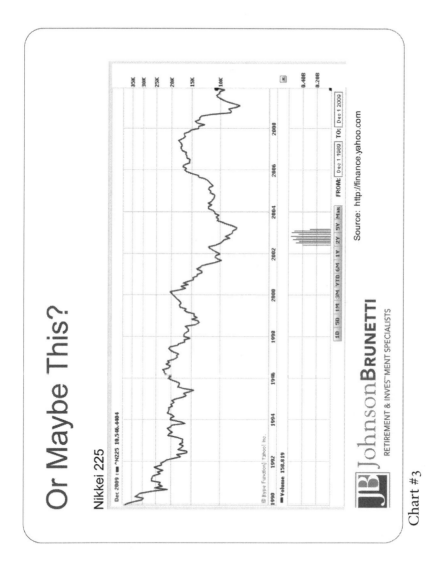

Source: http://finance.yahoo.com

Chart #3

Or Even This?

Dow Jones Industrial Average

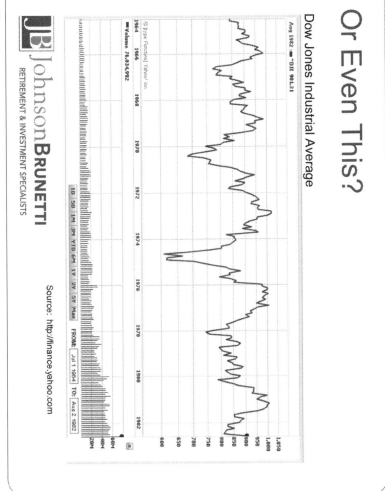

 Johnson**Brunetti**
RETIREMENT & INVESTMENT SPECIALISTS

Source: http://finance.yahoo.com

Chart #4

It's all about protecting principal, folks. The reality is that we have had multiple 15- to 20-year periods in this country when the market and things tied to the stock market did very little. This is why the indexing or passive management philosophy, the theory that you should just buy index funds because no one beats the market, just doesn't work for many people, not because it doesn't work, but because most people, (when seeing their money earning nothing for a period of time) will switch out of one strategy just to lock in losses, many times just before that strategy or that type of investment starts doing well again. Most investment categories work in cycles. The U.S. stock market will do well for some time, then fall out of favor while something else, real estate for example, does well.

My favorite way to position a portfolio for retirement is as follows: notice the circle chart here where you have 1/3 in equities, 1/3 in steady income accounts, and 1/3 in safe accounts. The 1/3 in safe accounts utilizes, depending on current rates, government bonds, fixed annuities, indexed annuities, CD's and indexed CDs, in combination for safety and guarantees. This produces a portion of your savings that offers you peace of mind.

The 1/3 that comprises alternative and steady income investments includes real estate, corporate bonds, preferred stocks, etc. These steady alternative accounts are designed to spin off a 4% to 8% cash flow with less fluctuation of principal compared to stock market-based strategies. The income can be spent or put in other investments for future income needs. They are not risk-free, just different from stocks and mutual funds.

The final 1/3 includes stocks, managed accounts, and mutual funds. The goal here is to grow this third by 10%. But if it doesn't work out that way, then we can provide all our income needs from the safe and steady part of the portfolio.

One last point on this subject: since the biggest concern among retirees in the United States is running out of money, when possible we can use insurance companies to guarantee all of their needed income. Think of it as building your own private pension. The old pensions that are less common today than they were 15 or 20 years ago really worked pretty well. You got a steady check every month. You didn't have to worry about outliving it. You could even have an option that allows your spouse to continue to enjoy that income after your death. Do you know that you can design a private plan that works just like that, and many of these plans will guarantee a 5% or 6%

income stream? If guarantees are from an insurance company, they are based on the claims-paying ability of that company. You should work with somebody who specializes in these products to design the proper strategy for you.

MARKET
Things sensitive to stock market volatility. Upside potential and downside risk.

STEADY INCOME
Accounts with steady income streams to generate regular income.

SAFE
Cannot lose principal or interest earned. Guaranteed by either the U.S. Government, FDIC, or insurance companies and their respective state guarantee funds.

CHAPTER 4

GREED-ENTITLEMENT-ARROGANCE
THE CULTURE OF WALL STREET

These are the three core characteristics that can be present with some on Wall Street, and it's really unfortunate. Let's talk about what Wall Street was originally meant to do: to be a stock exchange that allowed companies to raise capital by selling equity or stock in themselves. This is in itself a very noble concept. If my manufacturing company needs money to build a new plant, to expand, or to buy machinery, I can sell equity in my company, perhaps 10, 15, 25, 50%, or even more. Investors are able to purchase shares of my company, and I use that money to expand, to increase the value of the company. As the value of the company increases, the value of my ownership goes up, and so does that of the investors.

The second intention of Wall Street was to offer IOUs or bonds in companies. Instead of selling ownership in my company, I can sell IOUs. I can sell a bond and guarantee an investor an interest rate in addition to his principal back at a certain time.

So this was the idea of Wall Street: to raise capital so that businesses could expand and thereby increase their value by borrowing dollars or by selling equity and putting it back into the business, which would generate a higher rate of return than the cost of the capital. So what has happened on Wall Street? Wall Street has turned into a money machine. Those who are insiders, those who are part of the old boys' network if you will (and I say old boys carefully, but it is indeed mostly boys), are in a culture where we have seen the negative consequences of greed, entitlement, and arrogance.

Let's talk about greed. Think about the mortgage debacle that happened in 2006, 2007, and 2008. People were able to borrow money to buy a house without providing any documentation of income or employment. They could just make up numbers, put them down on a mortgage application, and get a mortgage. This happened because the profit and fees earned by making those loans were much higher than the actual risks. In fact, most of the time there was no risk to the lender because Wall Street was able to package those loans, collect a big fat fee, and then sell them to investors around the world—investors like you and me who had money in pension plans, and other investors including different countries and cities, endowments, and charities that put their money into these mortgage-backed securities or collateralized debt obligations called CMBs or CDOs, and what happened? There was no real value there. The whole system almost collapsed. The story is told in the movie 'Too Big to Fail'.

Let's think about who *really* got hurt by the mortgage debacle. Did Wall Street, which financed and created these vehicles, get hurt? Not really. Now you may say their stock prices got hurt, and that's true; they certainly took some losses. But look at the bonuses of the people who packaged and sold these products collected in 2005, 2006, and 2007, before the entire market imploded. Huge, extravagant bonuses. If you're a Wall Street executive who can collect $20 million or $30 million for packaging products that hurt the public, you can focus on the short-term, put the money in your pocket, and not worry about the long term.

Now let me be very clear here. I'm not saying, nor do I think that every executive who packaged those products thought the mortgage market was going to implode, but there were plenty of warning signs, and any time you throw that much money around in the form of commissions and bonuses to people for packaging products that might not have inherent value, you're going to have problems.

Now what we have is an American public whose house values went down. Jobs have been lost, and retirements have been postponed. Let's be clear: part of the reason house values have gone down is because their values at the end of 2006 were artificially high because of increased liquidity in the marketplace. But the bottom line is that we feel poorer, the market hurt, most of our 401(k)s went down, but the Wall Street fat cats are still fat.

Will this be the end of it? No, absolutely not. In the late 70s and early 80s, it was junk bonds. After that was the Internet bubble; companies were valued much higher than their real, intrinsic value.

Thankfully, through it all our economy worked, and the market correction was exactly that: a correction. Things were out of line, and that correction was needed. But the greed of Wall Street is something you need to understand. We should be aware of it because it infects your investments—not affects, *infects*—your investments. When you buy mutual funds or stocks, you need to be very aware that you are on a playing field that is stacked against you as an individual investor, and you better be aware of the costs and the fees and the maybe "backdoor" motivations of those producing and selling those products.

Does that mean every product is bad? Absolutely not. We've invested a lot of money for our clients in some of these Wall Street–created products, but you just need to be very careful. Once again, when something seems too good to be true, it probably is. Remember the Lehman Brothers, Bear Stearns, and the many other firms that either vanished or were forced to sell themselves.

Now let's talk about this sense of entitlement. What really drives this idea that people can hurt the public by their greed and not have a problem with it? How can they sleep at night? It's simply a sense of entitlement. Because they went to the right schools, because they grew up on the right coast, because they played lacrosse, because they had the right connections, they're entitled to make $3 million, $10 million, $20 million, and more. It may be this sense of entitlement that causes a problem on Wall Street. If I feel that I'm entitled to make a ton of money and it doesn't matter how much it hurts you because you just didn't grow up in the right family or go to the right school or attend the right church or synagogue, that's a problem, a problem that hurts all of America. America was built on the backs of workers, and those workers should benefit.

The other attitude that goes along with entitlement is arrogance, the arrogance of somebody standing up and saying that he is entitled to this amount of money because he created these products that fuel America. Well, maybe they do fuel America, but they also can hurt America when greed, entitlement, and arrogance run out of control.

So understand how the culture of Wall Street affects you as an investor. Wall Street is rewarded and makes money when you take risk. When you put your dollars in a Wall Street firm, you can be rewarded or you can be hurt. But make no bones about it folks; that firm makes a lot of money when your money is at risk. If everybody with an account at a big brokerage firm put money solely in CDs or Treasury Bills, do you think Wall Street firms would make enough money to keep their doors open and pay for that fancy office space they have? I'm not sure they would. There is no guarantee that your broker, employed at that big Wall Street firm, will make the fundamental change in your portfolio that may need to be made when your retirement comes.

At your retirement, I believe that some, maybe all of your money should be protected from loss. Retirement can be ruined just by worrying that you will run out of money.

I realize I've gone off on a bit of a rampage, but I am sick and tired of the greed, entitlement, and arrogance in this business.

Once again, there are good, honest people at investment firms - and there are some bad apples - just like in any business. The difference is that making the wrong decision with your money is much more costly than buying a car from a less than honest salesperson.

CHAPTER 5

WHO WANTS TO TAKE YOUR MONEY?

One of the most important considerations in financial planning is not just the rate of return you get on your investments or the security of knowing that your money will last as long as you live; it's keeping your money away from people or institutions that can take it. The purpose of this chapter is to go through some of the different people and entities out there that may want to get their hands on your money and take it from you and spend it in a way that you don't approve of or just simply take it away so you and your family cannot use it.

The first party we think of is the IRS, which can penalize people. What do I mean by that? Well, if you don't save enough money for retirement, you can simply go on Social Security and probably take part in all kinds of state and federal programs to help you pay for your retirement. You certainly don't have to pay for healthcare, one of the most important and costly expenses in retirement. Yet if you do a good job like our clients do in saving for retirement, the IRS is there to take anywhere between 10, 15, 25, maybe as much as *45 cents of every retirement dollar* that you would like to spend. That's right—up to 45 cents when you factor in the taxes on Social Security, income taxes, and state taxes, which we're about to discuss.

TAXES, TAXES, AND MORE TAXES

Let's talk about the different types of taxes. One, of course, is income tax. IRAs are talked about more in the chapter "The Knockout Punch to the Taxman." When you take money out of an IRA or a 401(k), it gets taxed by simply being added to your income. In this situation, you've saved money all your life, and now you begin to spend it. Well, you may have Social Security, you may have a pension, and let's say you take, $1,500 a month or so, $18,000 a year, out of your

IRA or 401(k). It's possible that you're going to pay income tax of anywhere between $3,000 and possibly up to $7,000 a year on that money. Think about that; think about how much time you spent trying to get a decent rate of return on your money. Let's say you average 7% over your lifetime. Well, you didn't really get to keep 7%, did you? Because when you take out the money, the IRS gets 33% of it, so you really get only 4.25%. The IRS is very, very happy because all of that time you spent saving in your IRA or 401(k), they were your partner. You just didn't know it then; they were a silent partner until you began taking money out. One of the most important things we can do is be tax-efficient with our investments. Remember, the IRS is there in line from an income tax standpoint.

Let's talk about the estate tax next. Legislation now puts a very high limit on the estate tax. The current federal estate tax only applies to assets approximately $11 million per person (2019). Unless you have a net worth over that amount you don't owe federal estate tax. For most of our clients, this does not apply. They are just good, average, hard-working Americans who did a great job of saving money and have investable assets of less than $2 million.

Now let's talk about state governments. In Connecticut, where I live, the state inheritance tax affects estates or net worths above $3.6 million, while the federal government taxes everything above $11 million. Well, in Connecticut, or anywhere in the northeast in this country and certainly on the West Coast, it is not very hard to have a net worth over $2 million. If you have $1 million in savings and you live for another 10 years or so in Connecticut and you own your home, chances are that between the value of your home, your pension, your IRAs, your 401(k)s, and your various investments and savings, it'd be very possible to have a net worth of more than $2 million. So this is an area that you need to plan for. Do not allow the state to take more money than they deserve because of improper planning.

Another area you can lose your money to is healthcare, including health insurance companies and health providers and, in particular, nursing homes. *The aging baby boomer population could ignite a 75 percent increase in the number of Americans older than 65 who will spend time in a nursing home. Based on this projection, this number would increase from 1.3 million in 2010 to about 2.3 million in 2030.*[1] What

---

1   Mather, M. (2016, January 13). Fact Sheet: Aging in the United States. Retrieved January 10, 2018, from https://www.prb.org/aging-unitedstates-fact-sheet/ Population Reference Bureau

does a nursing home cost? Well, I know the average cost for a nursing home in Connecticut is over $400 per day, which comes out to over $12,000 per month, adding up to roughly $144,000 per year! And this is for an average nursing home, not a Cadillac by any means. How would a couple pay for that? If somebody has an average amount of investment assets, it would probably leave the spouse who does not need the nursing-home care impoverished by the time his or her spouse in the nursing home died. So it's very important that we plan for this, and there are two ways. One is by buying different types of insurance policies. The good news is that the old long-term care insurance policies that involved paying premiums that we lose if we don't use them are not as popular as they used to be. There is a new and improved type of insurance policy that allows you to set money aside, and if you need nursing home care you have the long term care insurance and the nursing home insurance, but if you never need the nursing home care, *your family gets all that money back plus a return on the money!* So you want to investigate this new type of hybrid nursing home insurance.

The other important way of planning for elder-care asset protection, and we stress this with all of our clients, is by getting a *proper* attorney as soon as possible, like now. And please note my emphasis on the word *proper*. Most attorneys, unfortunately, at least those whom we have come across, will be glad to do work when it comes to asset protection, but they are not necessarily competent to do so. It takes a very strong character for somebody to say, "I can't do this work; I'm in over my head," as opposed to just collecting a fee. Well, the good news is that here in Connecticut, Massachusetts and across the country we know of a good network of high-quality elder-care attorneys who can protect your assets.

Now someone might say, "Wait a minute, Joel! Isn't there a five-year look-back if I give assets away before going into a nursing home that the government takes back?" Well, that's not exactly the way it works. That's why it's so important to educate yourself on these subjects. We can help you, and good elder-care attorneys can help you, but make sure you pick the right one and you get references. Once again, we have a network of such attorneys with whom we're very pleased. One of the attorneys we know who works very close to our office won a court case against the State of Connecticut, which was trying to recapture assets that his client had given away and put into an annuity before going into a nursing home. And so the good news is there are competent professionals out there.

The next group of people who may want to get your money are the people your kids have married. Now let's face it, moms and dads; we all love our kids, but sometimes we're not too sure about the people they marry. There could be a divorce, there could be a situation in which we leave money to our son, for instance, when we die, and then our son dies and his wife remarries. All of a sudden, the money we wanted to go to our child and our grandchildren ends up part of another marriage and possibly not getting to our grandchildren at all, or getting spread out among people who are not even in our bloodline. This is why it's so very, very important to work with a competent financial planner who works within a network or a team of attorneys who can help you structure your estate so that this won't happen.

Has anybody ever told you that you can control assets from the grave? The wonderful thing about a trust, if a trust is appropriate for you, is that you get to write the rules, and almost any rule that you want to impose either on your children or the people your children marry can be imposed. What we're talking about here is not trying to punish other people, not trying to be vindictive; what we're talking about here is good stewardship. *You've earned your money, you have certain values when it comes to money, and you deserve to have those values expressed, even when you're no longer here, and maybe for one, two, or three generations to come.* This can be done when it comes to your money. It's just a matter of proper estate planning.

Now let's talk about one other thing that I'm going to illustrate with a story. My family was on vacation in the Canadian Rockies and having a wonderful time. It's absolutely gorgeous scenery. In fact, the scenery is so stunning that at times when we would look out our hotel window or go for a walk and look up at the mountains, they almost didn't seem real because they were just so vivid, the air was so crisp, and the sky and the lakes were unbelievable. Well, there's also a lot of wildlife up there, bears, moose, and deer. We were having a wonderful time when one morning my 11-year-old Noah pulled me by the arm through the lobby and outside the hotel. He was so excited that I thought for sure he had seen a bear or a deer or elk and was going to show it to me. He's a real animal lover. Well, what does he see out in front of the hotel? A $280,000 Lamborghini, a car that'll go 220 miles an hour. Noah wanted his picture taken in front of that car. I'm no dummy. He loves cars, my oldest son likes cars, and I like cars too. But the last thing I want is for him to blow his inheritance on one or two of those cars after my wife and I pass away. We all know that sometimes our kids don't share our values with money. And so with Noah, if he continues his love of cars, if he continues to spend his allowance as quickly as he does on things like candy and so on, well, we might just put a provision in our will and in our trust that says he doesn't get a lump sum but perhaps a certain stipend every month for as long as he lives, and there would be other money available for certain things, like education or charitable giving. You can do this; it's control from the grave. The important thing is that you have certain values when it comes to your money, values that you want expressed in your estate plan.

One last little statistic I want to share with you, and this is so, so important for you to understand: most of the time, after both spouses die, their kids learn their IRA is cashed out completely. *The average inheritance in this country is spent very quickly.* Think about that when you plan your estate. Once again, do you have good kids or bad kids or both? I don't mean good or evil kids; I mean kids who are good with money and kids who are bad with money. Many of us have children who have challenges in life, and maybe there's a need to restrict some of those kids from getting money.

Another circumstance we see in our financial services practice: many of our clients have children with special needs. Sometimes it's a matter of severe retardation; other times it might be a form of autism; still other times it might be some sort of traumatic injury for which a child is getting some type of state aid. Generally, if somebody getting state aid inherits money, that event will disqualify them for that aid. The inheritance has to be spent on their care before they can go back on state aid. Hence the need for special-needs planning, a very, very critical matter. You can keep a special-needs child from being disqualified for state aid by setting up a special-needs trust. We've set up such trusts many times with the assistance of the attorneys in our network; this is a way you can make sure that a special-needs child is taken care of, that the inheritance is split equally and cannot be taken by the state.

Lastly, we live in a very litigious society. People sue other people and you may get sued. Get an umbrella insurance policy. My recommendation is at least $2,000,000 to protect your assets from a legal judgment.

This has been a chapter that talked briefly about some of the people who want to take your money. Folks, your money is *your* money; you should be able to control it and decide where it gets spent.

CHAPTER 6

THE TRUTH ABOUT MUTUAL FUNDS

Do you know the number-one way that Americans save for retirement and the number-one way that Americans invest while in retirement? You guessed it—mutual funds. Are mutual funds good or bad? Well, they're better than some alternatives, but there are some facts that can make mutual funds very problematic to own.

Deferred compensation plans, 401(k)s, 403(b)s, and even brokerage accounts are full of mutual funds. Many advisors use mutual funds to invest for clients, and these funds can be good or bad. How do you know that you have a good one? Do you know that over the long-term, according to Morningstar, many funds did not beat the benchmark that they are measured against? What are the chances that you have a good mutual fund?

We're going to explore in this chapter the problem with mutual funds, when they should be used and when they should not be used. To be clear—full disclosure here—we use mutual funds in some of the portfolios we manage for our retirement clients, but I am very careful to select mutual funds that, in our opinion, make sense for our clients. Here, however, is the problem: some advisors use mutual funds exclusively, and mutual funds can have very high expenses. Some of you are saying, "Well, I can buy an Index fund for instance, an index fund that charges only five basis points, $1/20^{th}$ of a percent, in expenses, maybe $1/10^{th}$ of a percent in expenses. That's a very low expense, Joel." That's correct; that's a very low expense, but index funds in my opinion can do fine in certain types of markets but very poorly in others. If you had an Index fund in 2008, your money was down approximately 35% to 40%! Most people, no matter how smart they are, will sell because they see their retirement going out of the window.

Now if you buy actively managed funds (of which I am a bit more of a fan), then you have other issues. One is that the expenses are much higher—1%, possibly 2%, in management fees. In addition to that are all kinds of other expenses not disclosed in the prospectuses because they are expenses of custody and trading. Our firm uses an analysis tool that gets to the root of what you're really paying, and you'd be surprised. Some mutual funds say they have a 1% expense ratio, but when analyzed and all the other costs are backed out, many times the cost of owning that fund is as high as 4%. What it means, folks, is that if you had $100,000, the holdings in that fund had to go up 4-5% ($4,000-$5,000), before you even broke even because of those expenses. These very high expenses and trading costs are one of the problems of mutual funds.

The second big problem with mutual funds is that the money managers, although they get paid for performance, they also get paid for the amount of assets they attract. Let me say that again: they are not only paid for performance, but they also get paid for the amount of assets they attract. Money managers of most mutual fund families are paid a certain percentage of the total assets under management. So instead of having the incentive to beat the market, they have the incentive to attract more dollars. This is why you see companies such as Fidelity, Vanguard, and T. Rowe Price doing so much advertising and marketing. It's all about attracting dollars, folks. So keep that in mind, the compensation structure in most mutual funds families may be rewarding the wrong outcome.

There are certain mutual fund families that I think really have it right when it comes to this compensation issue because they reward their managers for long-term performance, but please understand that attracting dollars to a mutual fund sometimes pays a lot more than making dollars in the market.

Here's another issue with large mutual funds: If a money manager wants to take a position in a stock because he believes in the company, he can't just buy enough stock to have a significant, positive impact on his fund in one day as you and I could. It takes them many weeks to build such a position in that stock because if he takes 1% to 2% of his fund's money and buys that stock in one day, he could move that stock up substantially, possibly out of the price range where he wants to own it. Think about how much can change, folks, in 6 to 10 weeks. This is a significant problem with popular funds; it can take far too long for a money manager to take certain positions in some stocks.

Let's think about the opposite of that. What if there's bad news about a company that makes a money manager want to get out of the company? That also might take 6 to 10 weeks. We saw an example of this in the dot com bubble; when it began to burst, people were pulling money out of Janus, a big mutual fund company. When Janus started selling its positions, it actually drove the market down because it had such a huge share of technology stocks. A mutual fund's size can affect its ability to sell as well as buy, and either can be problematic.

I mentioned earlier that we use certain mutual funds in some of our managed portfolios. I like mutual funds that allow me to bet on the manager rather than on the particular fund or fund company. Be aware of how expensive mutual funds can be, but then keep their costs in perspective: *Sometimes you get what you pay for.*

CHAPTER 7

WHY REAL ESTATE WORKS

In this chapter we'll address how and why real estate investing works. One of the reasons real estate works is that everyone needs somewhere to live and somewhere to work. You buy a house because chances are you don't want to sleep out on the streets. Well, there is a value in that home; it's residential real estate. If you own an apartment building, you rent out those apartments and in so doing you create income while owning an asset that may appreciate in value. What other kinds of real estate are there? How about office buildings? And consider warehouses, where companies store goods waiting to be sold.

Another reason why real estate works is that we're not making any more land. There is a limited supply of land.

A third reason that real estate works is that I can rent property and create cash flow. For example, if I spend $1 million on an apartment building I may be able to create perhaps a 10% cash flow with the rent. If it costs me only 4% to operate the building, then I pocket 6%. *You* do the math. Even if it costs me 6% to operate the building, I pocket a very nice 4% cash flow. If I use leverage in the form of a mortgage, I increase my cash flow.

Last but not least, real estate purchased for the right price can keep up with inflation. If my apartment building appreciates by 3% to 4% per year and inflation is 3-4%, I'm keeping up with inflation. When I sell that building someday, I'm going to get that much more than I put in, and I enjoyed the cash flow in the meantime. These are some of the reasons why real estate works. Much of the wealth in our country was created through real estate. Consider railroads, for instance; a tremendous amount of the share value of publicly traded railroads is due to the real estate they hold. The Sears bankruptcy is another example where one could argue that the main asset of the corporation is the real estate it owns and not the buying and selling of consumer goods.

Real estate developers have made money buying and developing real estate. I have clients who are real estate developers who may buy a piece of land, build and sell 12 houses, and make—if they do it correctly and well—a very, very nice profit. Real estate can offer tremendous returns on equity.

Another factor that makes real estate work is that we don't need to come up with all the cash to buy it. If I want to buy $1 million of General Motors stock today, I have to come up with $500,000 and borrow the other half (and pay interest on that) in order to control $1 million of General Motors shares. With real estate, I can put only 20%, sometimes less than that, in effect controlling $1 million worth of real estate for $200,000 or less. This gives me tremendous leverage. If that $1 million piece of real estate I'm controlling for $200,000 goes up 5% in value, the increase on my $200,000 is $50,000, a 25% return. You have to factor in interest rate costs here, but I think you get the idea. I talk in some of my seminars about how real estate investment trusts, which are basically funds of many different real estate properties, may generate a nice yield plus appreciate in value.

Real estate can be an inflation hedge. So when appropriate, some investors have put some of their money into mutual funds which invest in real estate companies. Sometimes these funds are referred to as REIT funds.*

You want to be very careful, though. You have enough liquidity to meet emergency needs, for instance, if the bank calls that loan or if interest rates spike and yours is an adjustable-rate loan. The purpose of this chapter is not to show you how to make money in real estate—there are plenty of books that do that. What the purpose of this book is for is to point out different ways that money works. And certainly real estate can work in a very advantageous way.

ONCE AGAIN, JUST TO REVIEW:

- Everybody needs somewhere to live and somewhere to work.
- They're not making any more land.

- If I own real estate, I can take out a very nice cash flow.

- Real estate purchased for the right price is a great inflation hedge.

---

*   *The real estate trusts we talked about still have risks associated, so one must be careful and make the time to understand how these investments can fit into his or her financial plan.*

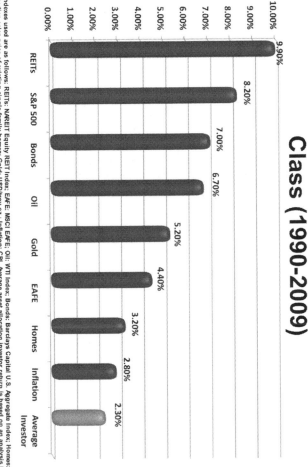

20-year Annualized Returns by Asset Class (1990-2009)

Asset	Return
REITs	9.90%
S&P 500	8.20%
Bonds	7.00%
Oil	6.70%
Gold	5.20%
EAFE	4.40%
Homes	3.20%
Inflation	2.80%
Average Investor	2.30%

Indexes used are as follows: REITs: NAREIT Equity REIT Index; EAFE: MSCI EAFE; Oil: WTI Index; Bonds: Barclays Capital U.S. Aggregate Index; Homes: median sales price of existing single-family homes; Gold: USD/troy oz.; Inflation: CPI. Average asset allocation investor return is based on an analysis by Dalbar Inc. which utilizes the net of aggregate mutual fund sales, redemptions and exchanges each month as a measure of investor behavior. Returns are annualized (and total return where applicable) and represent the 20-year period ending 12/31/09 to match Dalbar's most recent analysis.

Example of Real Estate Returns Compared to Other Assets

CHAPTER 8

THE ONE-PAGE ROADMAP FOR YOUR FINANCES

Have you ever read a financial plan prepared by a broker who works for a large financial firm? Typically these plans come in a big binder, are at least 80-plus pages long, and are very complicated. You know what happens when the prospective client takes these plans home after sitting for up to two hours going over the plan with the broker? Usually nothing.

The plan, too overwhelming for the client, doesn't get implemented. Why is this? It's just too much to do at once. In my many years of experience in the business of helping people make financial decisions, I have learned that for most of my clients, the best approach is to identify and solve one problem at a time. This is a much simpler approach. It benefits the clients in that most of them find it much easier to move forward.

The typical financial consultant who works for a large institution has been trained to put the whole plan together and present it at one time. They will say that the way I do things is "incomplete, malpractice, or just a way to create a number of financial transactions to get the client involved in."

Let's say you have the perfect financial plan written by two Ivy League PhDs who have 20-plus years of experience on Wall Street. The plan is on beautiful linen paper and presented in a beautiful leather binder. It has every possible contingency in life accounted for: retirement, college funding, special needs for grandkids, insurance planning, and tax planning. But *what good is the plan if it's too overwhelming for the client to implement*? My firm's one-page plan, the Money Map, helps alleviate this issue. It prompts a discussion about what's most important to the client, who is then able to choose which problem to solve first. Does every life problem get solved? Well, sometimes yes, sometimes no, but if we just solve the top three issues, in many of the cases we've done a better job than the broker who uses a complicated plan.

Let me tell you a little secret about the big plan put out by the big firm: Usually it's just a tool to impress the client; what the broker really wants to do is direct the conversation away from it as soon as possible so he can focus on selling you some type of financial product, whether it's mutual funds or insurance.

We've talked enough about what's wrong with the way some of the other guys do things. I like to stay as positive as possible here. These are the advantages of a SIMPLE plan:

- I get agreement on the problems to be addressed right away. It's up to the client to identify the most important problems. It's not about me and what I think is most important—I want to talk about what concerns the client has and address those problems first.

- Understanding is created because it is visual. Most people think in pictures. Therefore, the simple one-page plan gives people a roadmap, if you will, and a step-by-step process of what to address.

- Investment concepts are simplified for clients. For the first time, the disinterested spouse is not only engaged but also understands how investments work and so takes part in the process.

- By doing things one step at a time, decisions are simple and easy, and therefore the client situation is improved quickly. Everybody wins.

You would think that everyone in the business of giving investment advice would follow this simple approach to helping the public, wouldn't you? Well, that's not what is happening out there. Many advisors talk in financial jargon, confuse the client, and even exclude one of the spouses, all while trying to prove how smart they are. That process is broken, in my opinion. That process is not about the client at all but about how great the brokerage firm is and how smart the advisor is.

The process should be about the clients, their needs, and their goals. Once again, many on Wall Street have it backwards.

Each chapter in this book can be taken by itself to improve one area of your financial life. You do not need to read the entire book before you take action steps. How do you eat an elephant? One bite at a time. How do you secure your financial future? One step at a time. You will see the progress, feel peace of mind, and be encouraged to continue to take the next step. Remember, it's about progress, not perfection. You may never arrive at the utopia of a perfect financial life. Instead, you arrive at a place where your financial life is a reflection of your goals and values and an example to those you love and influence. Accept the fact that it won't be perfect, but by taking one step at a time and following the Money Map, by implementing our one-page plan, things can get better and it is likely you will gain some peace of mind and purpose with your finances.

Bob & Mary Example

401(k)	IRA	IRA	IRA	IRA	TAX
Emerson w/Vanguard	Thomaston Bank	Vanguard VWENX	Amer Funds	LPL MFs	Banking
Bob $1,159,998.00	Mary $7,146.00	Bob $242,583.00	Mary $14,400.00	Bob $409,785.00	Joint $165,000.00

1.99%
13 mo. CD

MONTHLY INCOME ANALYSIS

	Current	Future	
Bob Earned:	$21,249	$0	
Mary Earned:	N/A	N/A	Not working
Bob Pension:	$0	$2,850	
Mary Pension:	N/A	N/A	
Bob Social Security:	$0	$2,800	
Mary Social Security:	$0	$1,400	
Investments:	$0	$0	
TOTAL:	**$21,249**	**$7,050**	
GOAL:	$0	$15,000	

Concerns:

For both: "Retirement"
Out-living my money
Reducing current income taxes
Safety of principal, retirement & non-retirement money
Maximum investment return

Bob Target Retirement Date: Age 65
Mary Target Retirement Date: Age 64
Income Goal: $15,000
3/1/19

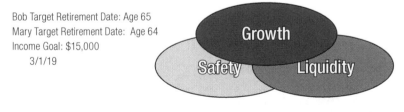

MONEY MAP
RETIREMENT REVIEW®
Doesn't your future deserve a second opinion?

☐ One Page Financial Plan
☐ Retirement Income Plan
☐ Portfolio Stress Test
☐ SS Income Maximization

401 (k)

AGENDA/ NOTES:
Review Riskalyze score
Investment overlap present?
Discuss life insurance contracts - cannibalizing itself?

Spouse 1 DOB=>   5/11/59
Spouse 2 DOB=>   8/15/60

TOTAL Net Worth (excluding primary residence): $1,998,912

Market: $1,826,766 = 91%

Alternative: $0 = 0%

Safe: $172,146 = 9%

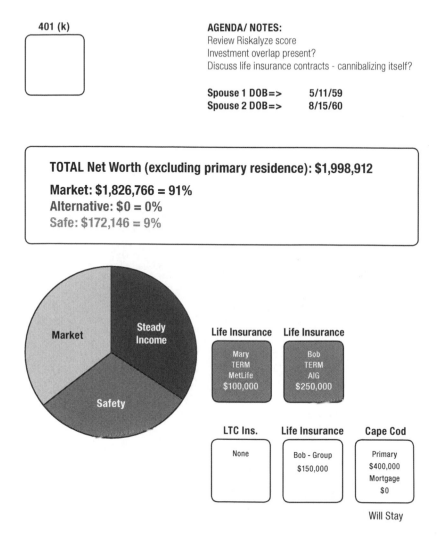

Market

Steady Income

Safety

Life Insurance

Mary
TERM
MetLife
$100,000

Life Insurance

Bob
TERM
AIG
$250,000

LTC Ins.

None

Life Insurance

Bob - Group
$150,000

Cape Cod

Primary
$400,000
Mortgage
$0

Will Stay

CHAPTER 9

THE MONEY MAP: YOUR ENTIRE FINANCIAL LIFE ON ONE PAGE

Your Money Map allows you to visualize your current financial situation. It's a great starting place to see your whole financial life on one page.

Let's start by looking at our example of the Money Map on the previous two pages. Please note that this Money Map is just an example and should not be construed as a personal recommendation.

In our example, we have Bob and Mary. You can see on the top right of the chart their ages - 59 and 60.

On the bottom left we have "concerns" listed. These may include things that Bob and Mary want to fix. They can also include things that Bob and Mary brought to our advisor's attention during their first meeting. Basically, all the things they want to make their financial planner aware of.

Under concerns, on the bottom left, we see Bob and Mary have stated that they want "Safety of Principal" on retirement and non-retirement money. They also want "Maximum Investment Return" with that degree of safety. At this point a good financial advisor will discuss the trade-offs between safety and maximum investment return and explain why it is not possible to have both - a balance is needed.

You also see at the very bottom of the left side that they want to rctire at ages 65 and 64 and have a total monthly income goal of $15,000.

Let's go back to the top right for a moment, where it says "Agenda". This lists the discussion points for the next meeting the financial advisor will have with Bob and Mary. At that meeting they will review the risk analysis of Mr. and Mrs. Example's investments, whether there is investment overlap (owning the same stocks in multiple mutual funds which can increase risk) and the problems with their current life insurance portfolio.

Let's pause for a minute here and make clear that this Map was prepared for Bob and Mary before they were clients. It is an example of their financial situation when they came to us. We use the Map as a guide in our meeting with them. The Map is used to help simplify their financial situation.

Look at the box on the left that says, "Monthly Income Analysis". On the left side of the box we have their current monthly income. On the right side, we have their projected income in retirement _before_ they take any income off their investments.

You can see that there is a shortfall between the $15,000 per month goal and the $7,050 per month they will get from pensions and Social Security.

If we move to the bottom right of the Money Map we have assets that are not for the purposes of generating retirement income. You can see 3 life insurance policies. There is also a box that shows they have no long-term care insurance and that their primary residence on Cape Cod with a value of $400,000 has no mortgage. There is a note underneath stating that they plan to stay there in retirement.

So far, you can see how the Map organized their goals, concerns, present situations and future plans.

Now, let's talk about the three graphics in color on the left side. Keep in mind that these are just concepts for illustrative purposes and not meant to be taken absolutely. The three bubbles on the left represent three ingredients you can have in any investment - Safety, Liquidity and Growth.

The idea here is that in most investments, you can only have two of the three ingredients. Think of an account at a bank. You have safety and liquidity, but no growth potential. A stock or mutual fund portfolio has growth potential and liquidity, but you give up safety of principal.

Lastly, a fixed-index annuity has safety of principal and more growth potential than a bank deposit, but you give up some (not all) of your liquidity. In reality, the annuity is liquid, like a CD is liquid, but with a penalty if you don't hold it to term.

The idea of the 3 bubbles is to illustrate a trade-off, you must give up one to get the other 2.

Most investors should have a variety of accounts fit into all 3 possibilities.

A) Giving up growth for safety and liquidity

B) Giving up liquidity for growth and safety

C) Giving up safety for growth and liquidity

The blend or allocation between the 3 should be adjusted for the unique needs of the individual.

On the right side of the Map is a pie chart. The pieces of the pie are Safety, Market, and Steady Income.

Once again, we have a discussion with the client to discuss different options that fit into each category. For example, a stock would fall into the Market category. A ten-year treasury bond would be in the Safe category (although, you could lose money on a 10-year government bond if you sell it before it fully matures.) Real estate and corporate bonds would fall in the Steady Income category.

Across the top of their Money Map are boxes that have their different accounts entered into them. In the right center of the Map, you see Bob and Mary's total investable assets. Excluding their primary residence, they have $1,998,912.00.

The "Market", "Alternative and Safety" lines under that show the amount of money Bob and Mary have in each category. These, of course, are the same categories we see on the pie chart.

You will notice that 91% of their money is in the Market category. 91% of their money could go down in value when the market or the underlying investments go down.

Based on the previously-discussed points with Bob and Mary, they are probably taking more risk than they will be able to handle without reacting to a market downturn and having an adverse outcome on their financial plan.

Remember, one of the biggest risks to an investor is how they behave in times of stress and worry. Most people do the wrong thing at the wrong time.

Bob and Mary need roughly a 5% rate of return on their investments to cover their income shortfall identified in the "Monthly Income Analysis" on the left side of the Money Map.

A 5% return means they probably need to accept some exposure to the stock market, but they could certainly benefit from building in some safety to protect against bad times. What is the correct mix of safety and risk? That is what should be decided at the second meeting with their financial advisor.

Picture your own Money Map or better yet build your own. If you want, we will build your Map for you. From my experience, most people I talk to love having a visual, simple picture of their financial situation.

CHAPTER 10

IT'S ALL ABOUT INCOME

Most people stumble through life not knowing what they really want or need. —*Joel Johnson*

What is retirement planning? It has many definitions. For the purpose of this book I will define retirement planning as defining how your ideal life looks after you no longer have to work, and then making a plan to get to this ideal life.

I want you to notice a few key points in the definition. First, there is no age associated with retirement. The most fulfilled people I know, some of whom are 65, 70, even 75, are people still making a significant contribution to others. In fact, you could say that they haven't retired. So let's define retirement as the age at which someone *could* retire but may choose to continue working. For some, that may be working at a company, or consulting, or volunteering somewhere, but they are still active. So now that we know that there is no specific age related to our definition, let's talk about the other important components to this unconventional description of retirement.

The second aspect is freedom. We no longer need to work at a job to earn money, but we may choose to work to earn money. We'll come back to this later.

Third, it is important to know with clarity what you want this stage of your life to look like. Do you want to see your children and grandchildren every week? Do you want to travel frequently? Where will you live? What country will you live in? Will you do the yardwork? See all the possibilities here? Start with a clean slate and create your ideal life.

Here's the most important question: What are all these dreams dependent on besides your health? You've got it—money. But wait; the answer isn't just *money*. That's too simplistic, too vague. The answer is *income*.

You need steady, predictable income that will meet all your needs. Why is it important to think this way? Because I have seen investment portfolios that have been managed poorly and have created insecurity, uncertainty, and anxiety for clients. You can imagine how this affects retirement; you're always a little worried, a little anxious that your money may run out.

My firm, on the other hand, creates investment portfolios designed to produce predictable income, contingency or emergency money, and growth to protect against inflation. We also strive to find products and investments that will guarantee the income clients need so they don't have to worry about running out of money and can concentrate on their ideal life.

Can this be done? Well, if you have saved enough money, it can be, but you must avoid the mixed messages and erroneous information coming from some in the financial services business. We've been brainwashed against the very products and investments that can create this predictable income. Let's take the conventional wisdom: How much income should you take out of a retirement portfolio every year? Most say 4%. Wow. That may not be very exciting. Many times those that use this "4% rule" are talking about creating a portfolio of mutual funds to achieve this.

This explains why they're scared of saying you should take more than 4%. This begs the question: Okay Mr. Broker, do you guarantee that as long as I don't take more than 4% from my investments I won't run out of money? No. They won't guarantee anything. In fact, some will say based on a Monte Carlo analysis (an overly complex mathematical analysis based on millions of probable outcomes) that there is a 10% probability that you will run out of money. That's horrible. A 4% cash flow and you still may run out of money? You need $1 million to create $40,000 of income, and even that's not guaranteed.

Let's talk about the investments some say you're supposed to avoid at all costs. You know, the ones that the brokers say are costly rip-offs with high fees and commissions, the ones the brokerage firms bash and the mutual fund companies bash, those that some of the talking heads slam. For instance, let's take annuities. There, I said it—those annuities that we've been told not to buy, to stay away from because they're horrible. What's an annuity? It is a tool that can guarantee income, one that, if properly designed by an expert, can guarantee you a 5% to 6% income stream for the rest of your life with no potential for running out of money, and also with potential raises.

You say, "Wait, Joel—6%?"

Yes, 6%, with a guarantee. It's really interesting that the very same mutual fund companies that say annuities are bad cannot guarantee a 4% income without you running out of income. The insurance company that the brokerage firms, mutual funds, and some unknowing industry pundits warn you to stay away from can guarantee you that 6% income. Gee, I wonder why those firms hate annuities? I'll leave you to figure that out.

Now, keep in mind that you may spend some or all of the account down to zero, but you may also take the portfolio of mutual funds down to zero. The difference is that if the annuity goes to zero, the insurance company will still send you checks, as long as you're alive. If you spend your mutual funds down to zero, your income stops. Let's talk about another way to get guaranteed income. Some say bond funds. No, no, *no*. There is a use for bond funds. I use them from time to time, but there is a much better way to create income. Guaranteed income, you ask me? Well, you tell me when I'm done explaining.

Pick some American or international companies that you think will not go out of business before you die.

Who are they? I was born in 1962, so let me pick a few for myself that I don't think will go out of business before I die: General Electric, Walmart, Exxon Mobil, Shell Oil, Chevron, Prudential Insurance, MetLife, Google, Apple, Wells Fargo, JPMorgan, and Goldman Sachs—you get the idea. Do you know that right now (1/1/2019) Wells Fargo bonds are paying between 3% to 5%? This means that if I put a portion of my money with Wells Fargo, they will guarantee me, for example, 3% to 5% interest for 10 to 20 years. The only way I lose that money is if Wells Fargo breaks its guarantee and is forced into bankruptcy. That may or may not happen. As long as Wells Fargo stays out of bankruptcy, I get my 3% to 5%, whatever the current yield to maturity was when I bought the bond. Furthermore, my principal is guaranteed by Wells Fargo.

You know, what if I used a combination of bonds from the companies I listed previously? I could create a nice yield and have my money guaranteed by those particular companies.

How about a combination of annuities and bonds? I can design the annuities to give me raises for my inflation protection and use the bonds for a slightly higher but nonetheless level income. Are you getting the picture here? Could this be something that Street doesn't want to seem better than its prepacka, products that they make so much profit on? One again, you decide.

Now, before we move on to the next income-producing product, let me say that you should consult an expert before doing this yourself, because one misstep and you'll be stuck with something that could hurt you in the long run. You can pay someone 1% to 1.5% and let them be on the hook to create your portfolio for you. It may be well worth it. Those who want to save the 1% to 1.5% by doing it themselves are playing in a game that they may not understand. In fact, may not even know who their real competitors are. It's a little bit like a high school football team going out on the field to face the Chicago Bears or the Green Bay Packers. Let me know how it goes next time you decide to operate on yourself to save that small fee you would've paid the doctor, the expert. I think you get the idea here.

Last but not least, let's talk about real estate. Now, we cover why real estate works in another chapter, but for now, just ponder this. You can buy a real estate investment trust that will create 2% to 4% income for you and give you inflation protection. Once again be

...l and use an expert, this is not without risk, but ...sider what we've said so far in this chapter.

- Define your ideal retirement using my definition.

- Understand that it's all about the income.

- With the tools I've mentioned, here is the choice: Give a Wall Street firm $1 million and listen when they tell you that you should take $40,000 a year out; you still might run out of money. On the other hand, give the right firm that $1 million; a properly structured plan may give you $60,000 a year in cash-flow and possibly a guarantee of never running out of money if the right products are used. The $60,000 is a 50% raise over the $40,000. Which would you rather have? If income is important to you, along with guarantees, then there may be better ways to achieve that through the old Wall Street way. Insurance product guarantees are based on the claims-paying ability than through of the insurance company.

CHAPTER 11

INVESTMENTS DESIGNED TO PRODUCE INCOME

In this chapter we'll discuss securities and other financial products that produce a steady, predictable income that some advisors ignore. Don't get me wrong. My firm reviews clients' statements when they come to get that second opinion from us, and many times we see portfolios with some of these securities that are being used the proper way. However, many other times we see a portfolio of mutual funds created by brokers trying to produce everything, including income with those funds, and in my opinion are missing the boat as far as safety and predictability of their income.

cuss securities that produce that steady income of our retired clients are looking for. Please also e that just because a security is an income-based ecurity or product, it does not mean somebody has to take the income. Many of our clients like these products because they simply produce a nice cash flow as an individual stock without as much fluctuation in principal.

The first security we'll talk about is the corporate bond, many of which are readily available to investors. To keep things simple here, a bond is simply a company's IOU. In the case of a corporate bond, your money is as safe as the company's promise to pay and its stability. In my opinion, an IOU from a strong blue chip company like a JPMorgan, or some other strong financial institution is a pretty solid promise to pay. I'm in my 50's as I write this, and I don't believe that a company such as JPMorgan—or other companies of that caliber—will go out of business before I die - of course, I could be wrong. If I can pick up a JPMorgan IOU that says it will pay me 4% interest for the next five to ten years, and on top of that get all my principal back at the end of that time, I feel pretty confident.

I reviewed some of our portfolios while preparing to write this chapter and saw that there are bond ETFs or funds that are paying approximately 4% interest, a very healthy interest rate in this current environment, when 10-year U.S. Treasury bonds are paying in the 2-3% range.[2]

Speaking of U.S. Treasuries, I want people to understand that you can lose money with United States bonds. If you buy a 10-year U.S. Treasury bond, which is a promise to pay from the US Government, it may pay, for the purpose of this example, 2.8% interest, and if interest rates climb—let's say they climb 3%—new treasuries would be paying 5.8%. Do you think that a 2.8% treasury bond is worth as much as one that pays 5.8%? Of course not. The 2.8% bond's value goes down. If you have to sell the bond before it matures, guess what? It is now worth only about 80-90 cents on the dollar. That's right; you can lose 20% of your money in a U.S. Treasury bond. The only way to get all your money back is to hold that bond until maturity. You have to be very careful.

Let's revisit bonds from strong companies (as of 1/1/2019). Exxon, Pfizer or 3M are companies whose

2   (GIFAX) As of 1/1/2019, the Guggenheim Floating Rate strategies fund has an S.E.C. yield of 4%. This is not a recommendation to own this particular bond, nor is it suggestive of a typical return.

bonds may be a good value. Please do not run right out and buy these bonds; by the time you're reading this it will have been at least a few weeks if not a year or more from the time of this writing, and the environment could have changed. One of the attractive things about corporate bonds is that you can sell them on any trading day at whatever is their current price—they're completely liquid. As long as I'm not holding hundreds of thousands dollars in one bond in a client's portfolios, I can sell them pretty much without a wrinkle.

Let's talk about another income-producing security: preferred stocks, which can be a little more volatile than corporate bonds as far as price movement goes. Many companies issue preferred stock as well as common stock. The difference between preferred stock and common stock is simple. The dividends on a preferred stock are "preferred" over the dividends on that same company's common stock. Let's use AT&T as an example. Right now AT&T pays a dividend on its common stock, so I can get that dividend quarterly, and if the stock goes up in value, I make even more money. If AT&T has a preferred stock, it cannot cut or stop the dividend on it until it completely quits paying dividends on its common stock—it's in that sense that one stock is "preferred" over the other. So it's a pretty fair assumption that if a company's common stock is paying a 4% dividend, my preferred stock may pay a 5% to 6% dividend, a dividend that is more predictable.

Let's think about this for a minute. We have the rest of the brokerage world, using mutual funds to produce income. And yet those mutual funds, as we've already seen, have holding costs and all kinds of trading fees, can be tax inefficient, and on top of that, the income they generate can be less productive.

Compare this to preferred stock issued by a quality company. It may pay a dividend and has liquidity with no hidden costs.

The only cost you're going to pay is if you're working with a financial advisor which, once again, we recommend highly. You pay a management fee to that financial advisor to watch over your portfolio and to deliver additional value.

Next, let's talk about REITs—real estate investment trusts. Real estate investment trusts can also provide an income that may be appropriate for a retiree's investment portfolio. Instead of being backed by a promise to pay like a corporate bond, or an equity issue like a preferred stock, a REIT is backed by real estate. (Some REITs are also backed by mortgages, which are of course indirectly backed by real estate.) Someone who has a mortgage doesn't own the real estate directly, but if he fails to pay on that mortgage, the underlying real estate can be repossessed.

Real Estate trusts typically pay out an income stream in the form of a dividend. Real estate trusts trade actively on an exchange and their price fluctuates every day. If the value of the real estate goes up over time, then the value of the share price may go up as well. This can be an appropriate income-producing security for a portion of your portfolio.

The Big Three

You Pick TWO!

Safety · **Liquidity** · **Growth**

- Of course, we want all three options, but life doesn't work that way.

- Most retirees find <u>Growth Potential</u> and <u>Safety of Principal</u> to be the most important.

- That means giving up some liquidity; but that's ok because our **core** nest egg *doesn't really need it!*

JB Johnson**Brunetti**
RETIREMENT & INVESTMENT SPECIALISTS

So far we've covered corporate bonds, preferred stocks, and of real estate investment trusts. So let's turn to a certain type of annuity. We refer to it in our practice as the *hybrid income plan*. Why would we use an annuity to generate income? One reason is that annuities were originally designed as income-generating products. Many people put money in them for a while and then take the money out without ever annuitizing them or using them for income, but the annuity was designed as an income vehicle.

When you "annuitize" an annuity, you lose control of the principal; however, you can use an annuity as an account where you earn an interest rate and take money out as needed without giving up access to your principal. There are a lot of bad annuities out there— you have to be very, very careful. Again, I would urge you to consult with a financial expert. A properly designed annuity can offer some very interesting features. You can put money into an annuity and for every year you leave the annuity alone, the value of your income account grows by anywhere between 6% and 8%.[3] Put $100,000 in, and the income value can be guaranteed to go to $200,000 in ten years. Now it

---

3   The income account value is not your regular account value that you can cash out. The income account value is the value that a lifetime guaranteed income is calculated from.

could be better than this, but let's just say it doesn't do any better than that and we just get the guarantee. My $100,000 could grow to $200,000 in ten years, at which time I could start taking out a guaranteed income stream that I would not outlive. So on that $200,000, someone who is 70 may receive a 6% guaranteed annuity with many of these hybrid income products.

Does this mean that the investor gives up control of the principal as was the case with the old annuities? Many of you have heard, "Don't put money into an annuity; when you die, the insurance company keeps the money." That's not the way these new and improved annuities, these hybrid income plans, work. The insurance company does not keep the money. If there's any money left in the account upon your death, your heirs get it.

So let's go through this. I put in $100,000 at age 60. The income account value is guaranteed to be at worst $200,000 when I turn 70. Now I begin to take an income stream of 6% from the annuity, $1,000 per month, $12,000 per year. That's a pretty good return from my original $100,000 investment. I can continue to take that $1,000 per month, and even if the account does not earn 7% for the first 10 years or 6% thereafter, and I live so long that the account value goes to zero because I've spent all the money, all the growth plus the original principal—if I'm still alive, the insurance company guarantees that I will continue to get my monthly checks. I can't outlive my money.

Remember earlier in the book we discussed the biggest fear for retirees, outliving their money? The problem in the old days was when we bought an annuity, we'd get a lousy 4% to 7% payout rate, but when we'd die, the insurance company kept any money that was left over. Well, that's not how hybrid income annuities work, so they can be very, very attractive ways of producing income.

I own two annuities called indexed annuities. They have no fees, and my principal is not at any risk. In the years when the stock market goes up, I get a portion of that upside of the market—not all of it, but a portion. In return for my giving up some of the market's upside, the insurance company takes away all of the downside.

Sounds good, but there is a catch. After all, there is no such thing as a free lunch.

I made a time commitment with my money. For the first ten years of the account I can take out 10%

without a penalty. After ten years I can take out 100%. My interest is calculated based on the performance of an outside index (S&P 500) but since I am guaranteed not to lose money, I do not get all the upside of the S&P 500.

The chart called "Market Performance" shows the performance of an index annuity. The circled lines are the annuity. The line with the most fluctuation is the S&P 500. You will notice that when the S&P 500 goes up, the annuity does not go up as much, but when the S&P 500 goes down, the annuity stays right where it is.

Fixed Index Annuity: Preservation & Accumulation

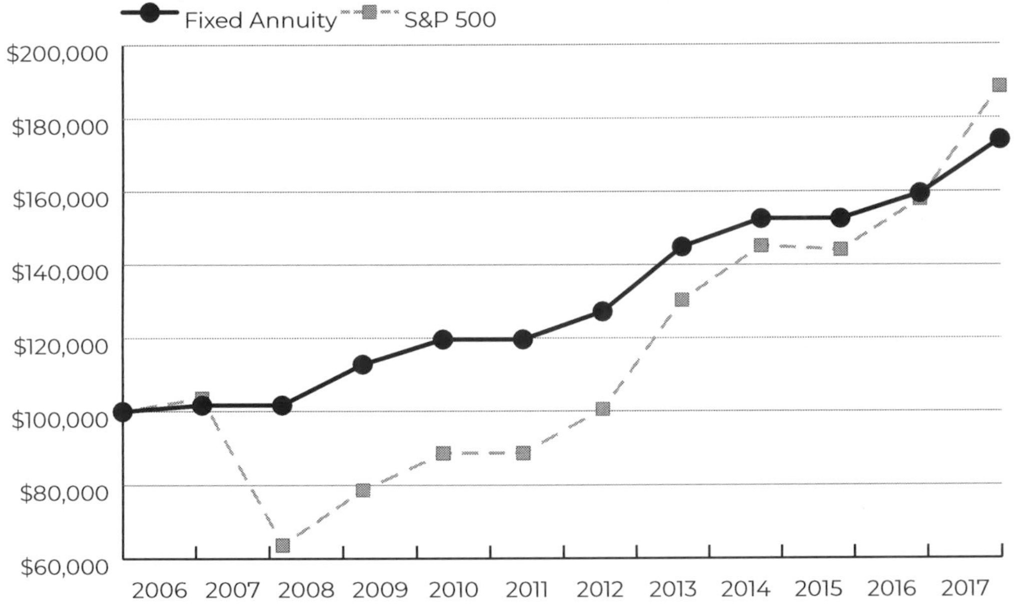

Fixed Annuity
S&P 500
$200,000
$180,000
$160,000
$140,000
$120,000
$100,000
$80,000
$60,000
2006
2007
2008
2009
2010
2011
2012
2013
2014
2015
2016
2017

All returns are hypothetical. This hypothetical demonstration assumes $100,000 initial premium into both and indexed and fixed annuity with a minimum guaranteed interest rate of 1% and no withdrawals taken. **Past performance is not an indication of future results.** Please call your financial advisor for information on product availability. Data Source: American Equity Investment Life Insurance Company.

The purpose of this chapter was to give you ideas about different income-producing securities. We have found in our practice at Johnson Brunetti that if we can deliver to clients between 4% to 6% income with steady principal, and in addition to that create other pieces of their portfolios that are protected. For many people, this strategy is more preferable than using 100% mutual funds or stocks to accomplish their goals.

CHAPTER 12

THE KNOCKOUT PUNCH
TO THE TAXMAN
THE ROTH IRA VERSUS TRADITIONAL
RETIREMENT PLANS

Imagine being able to take a chunk of your money and remove it from the reaches of the government forever. Would you like to do that? Would that benefit you and your family?

In this chapter we will explore the differences between Roth IRAs and traditional retirement accounts such as 401(k)s, 403(b)s, 457s, and traditional IRAs. Do you think taxes are going up? Are you concerned that your children will have to pay big taxes on your retirement accounts when they inherit that money? Are you bothered by the government attacking your retirement accounts when you turn 70 1/2? Roth IRAs allow you to avoid all of these problems.

There are two ways to get money into a Roth IRA. First, if you have earned income and your adjusted gross income is below the IRS limit, you can contribute money to a Roth IRA, 50 years old or more, you can contribute more money. Now the maximum AGI is less than $118,000 if you file single or $186,000 if you file married and jointly. Let me just state that again: you can contribute $5,500 to a Roth IRA if you're married and you file jointly as long as your adjusted gross income is not more than $186,000. If you're over 50, filing married, and your income is less than $186,000, then you can contribute $6,500. The limits noted are for 2017, but they typically do not change more than about 10% at the most per year. You can decide how applicable this is to you and simply get the current numbers online.

The second way that you can get money into a Roth is through a conversion from a traditional retirement account such as a 401(k), a 403(b), or an IRA. The catch here is that the amount I convert from a traditional retirement account to a Roth needs to be added to my income, so income taxes will be owed. For example, if I convert $200,000 from a traditional IRA to a Roth

IRA, I will add the $200,000 to my income in the year that I convert. That's the bad news.

The good news is that the $200,000 I converted will grow tax free as long as I leave it in the Roth. If I leave it alone for 20 years, at a 7.2% average annual return over that period, my $200,000 will be worth $800,000, and I can now spend the $800,000 tax-free.

The following charts and explanations illustrate three ways to handle a Roth conversion and the tax cost of each. If you think taxes are going up and you want to keep the government out of your future retirement savings, and if you're able to leave that money alone for a while, it probably would benefit you to convert to a Roth IRA.

SO THESE ARE THE THREE DIFFERENT WAYS TO CONVERT TO A ROTH.

- You can pay taxes from the current IRA while you convert it.

- You can pay taxes from outside the IRA that's being converted.

- You can pay no taxes by using nonretirement money to invest in a special tax-advantaged investment program, thus offsetting the taxes.

- You can pay the tax from life insurance proceeds, in a sense using someone else's money to pay the taxes.

On the following charts I will illustrate the differences between the four different strategies.

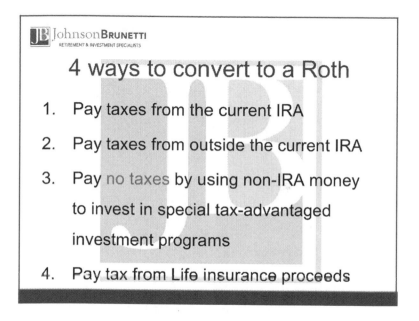

Strategy number one involves paying taxes from the current IRA. In our example here, Joe Torre, former manager of the New York Yankees and Los Angeles Dodgers, takes $200,000 out of his IRA and converts $150,000 of it to a Roth. He sets aside the other $50,000 to pay the taxes. As we can see on our chart, the $150,000 at 7% grows over 10 years to $295,000, and over 20 years to $580,000, while the government gets $50,000 in taxes. The good news is that Mr. Torre, if he's alive 20 years from now, can use that $580,000 and spend it in one lump sum if he wanted to completely tax-free. If he passes away, the $580,000 is inherited by his beneficiaries, and they can spend the money completely tax-free or leave it in a Roth IRA to continue to grow for their beneficiaries. Those beneficiaries have to take out a little bit each year, but it's not much; the majority of the money can grow tax-free.

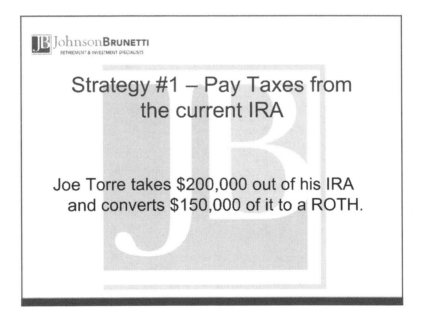

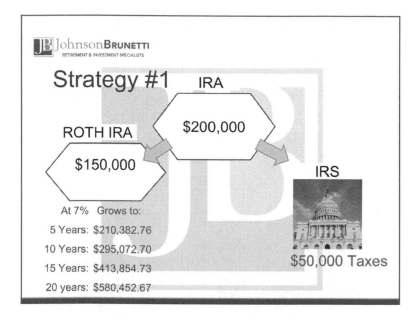

Strategy number two calls for paying taxes from outside the current IRA. This gives us the ability to convert the entire $200,000 IRA. So in this example, Red Sox former manager Terry Francona takes $200,000 out of his IRA and converts it all to a Roth, using other funds to pay the $50,000 in taxes. That $200,000, at 7%, grows in 20 years to $773,000. There's a big difference by leaving that $50,000 inside the Roth IRA and paying IRS taxes from another source. The chart that compares strategy number one to strategy number two demonstrates that the difference by paying the taxes from outside funds is almost $100,000 after 10 years and is almost $200,000 after 20 years. That's the power of dollars compounding tax-free inside the Roth IRA.

The lesson here on strategy number one versus strategy number two: it always makes sense to pay the taxes from outside the IRA being converted if possible.

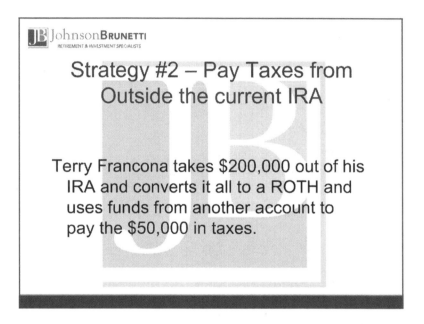

Strategy #2 – Pay Taxes from Outside the current IRA

Terry Francona takes $200,000 out of his IRA and converts it all to a ROTH and uses funds from another account to pay the $50,000 in taxes.

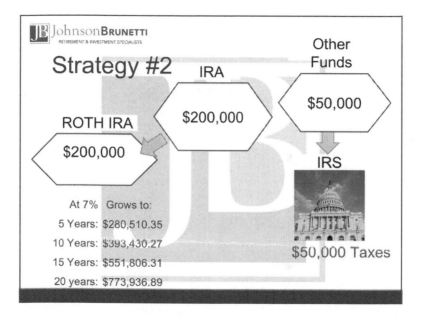

Strategy #1 Vs. Strategy #2

	Strategy #1	Strategy #2
At 7%, grows to:	Taxes Paid from INSIDE	Taxes Paid from OUTSIDE
5 years	$210,382.76	$280,510.35
10 years	$295,072.70	$393,430.27
15 years	$413,854.73	$551,806.31
20 years	$580,452.67	$773,936.89

Now strategy number three is conversion to Roth but zeroing out the taxes. In this example let's use George Steinbrenner, an interesting fellow who owned the Yankees of course for many years, and his family still controls the ball club. He hated taxes so much that he decided to die in 2010, the one year we had no inheritance taxes. Mr. Steinbrenner's net worth was estimated to be $1.6 billion. If he had died in 2011, his money would have been taxed at a much higher rate, and if he had died in 2009, his money would have been taxed at a very, very high rate. But as he died in 2010, his $1.6 billion passed tax-free to his heirs, while had he died in 2011, his estate taxes would have been approximately $550 million—a huge difference.

In this example, Mr. Steinbrenner takes $200,000 out of his IRA and converts it to a Roth IRA. He uses funds from another account to invest in a tax-advantaged oil and natural gas program, or a conservation easement which alllows a deduction that zeroes out the taxes.

Let's go over this example on the chart that illustrates strategy number three. Mr. Steinbrenner's entire $200,000, at 7% interest, grows to $773,936.89, as is the case with strategy number two. But he also takes money from another account and puts it into a program that provides a tax write-off of 60%-300% or more. So he puts $200,000 of income on his tax return because of the Roth IRA conversion but subtracts $200,000 (for example) of income because of the deduction for investing in the oil and gas program, or the conservation easement—thus completely zeroing out the taxes.

One benefit of the oil and gas program is that it creates monthly income after about a year that could last for years.

A word of caution here: investigate thoroughly any oil and gas program, or the conservation easement, as they are not for everybody; you need to be an accredited investor to get involved in all the programs I know about. The primary definition of an accredited investor is someone with a net worth of $1 million.

A second word of caution—really a word of *warning*—is that there are good operators and bad operators in the oil and gas, and in the conservation easement business.. Consult with a financial professional who has been investing in these programs for clients for quite some time so that you can get expertise on which programs may be appropriate for you. Be very careful with these oil and gas programs. You could lose all your money.

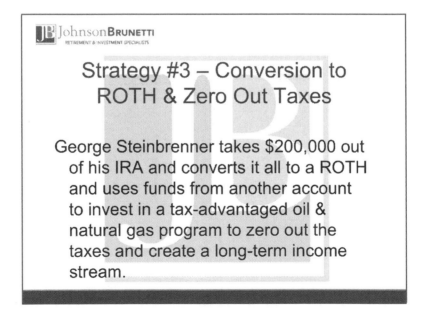

JohnsonBRUNETTI
RETIREMENT & INVESTMENT SPECIALISTS

Strategy #3 – Conversion to ROTH & Zero Out Taxes

George Steinbrenner takes $200,000 out of his IRA and converts it all to a ROTH and uses funds from another account to invest in a tax-advantaged oil & natural gas program to zero out the taxes and create a long-term income stream.

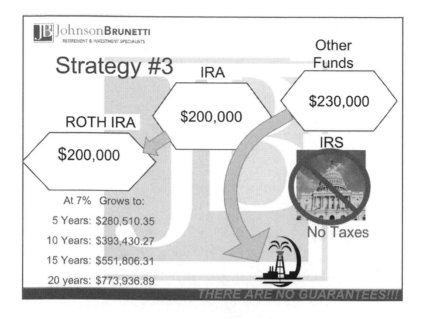

Strategy number four is a little different. In this case, instead of doing a Roth conversion today, we're going to defer that Roth conversion. In this example we use Ty Cobb and Mrs. Cobb. Ty is a real stickler; he doesn't want to pay any taxes before he has to. So Ty tells Mrs. Cobb that he is going to buy a life insurance policy so that when he dies, she will have cash to convert his entire IRA, because life insurance cash is tax-free. Strategy number four, then, shows that the $200,000 IRA grows at 6% to $641,000 when Ty Cobb dies at 85. Notice that we have a growth rate of 6% here, because he's going to extract 1% per year from the IRA to pay for the life insurance policy that will go tax-free to Mrs. Cobb when he dies. These proceeds are more than enough to pay the taxes and convert the entire $641,000 to a Roth IRA, and she has her $641,000 tax-free forever to use as she needs it or to pass on to her children.

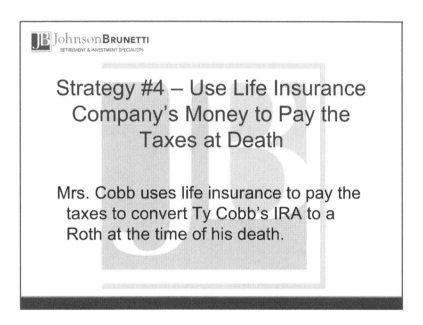

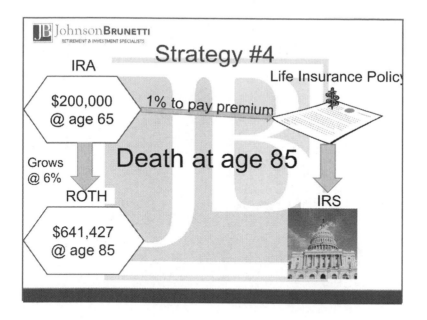

The key point with these four strategies on converting to a Roth IRA is that if you think taxes are going up and you want to take control of your taxes by locking in current rates, a Roth conversion is probably something to seriously consider. Once again, consult a financial professional, because there are many different moving parts to this Roth IRA conversion, and you want to make sure you have examined all the options and have chosen the correct one for you.

CHAPTER 13

HOW TO CHOOSE THE RIGHT FINANCIAL ADVISOR

In this chapter I will list nine things you may want to consider when you look for a financial advisor to work with. It is important that there is "chemistry" between you, that there is a good fit and a sharing of values. There also should be a feeling that the person understands you. We'll go over these elements in this chapter. Full disclosure here: The advisors at my firm, Johnson Brunetti, fit all of these characteristics. These are not the only characterists to consider, they are simply a few things that you may find important. If a financial advisor does not fit the description here, that does not mean that they are not worthy of consideration.

1. INDEPENDENT

I believe it is very important that the financial advisor you choose be independent, someone who is not an employee of a large firm. There are many firms at which brokers and advisors can work. I started in the business in 1989 as an employee of a big brokerage firm, and we employees were told what products and funds to recommend. We were told that what we had to sell was appropriate for everyone. When our sales manager had certain stocks that he would decide we should push in a certain month, guess what? Those stocks were what most people ended up owning.

I soon came to realize that this was the wrong approach, but unfortunately it still goes on today. Let's take for example a very large Wall Street brokerage firm. First of all, if you work for such a firm, the people you work with are employees of that firm, so their primary responsibility is to that firm, not to you. Their job is to increase shareholder value for that particular firm.

But if you work with an independent financial advisor, then you are the only person to whom that advisor answers. An ethical independent financial advisor does not have an agenda or a list of stocks to push. It is very important that you find an independent financial advisor.

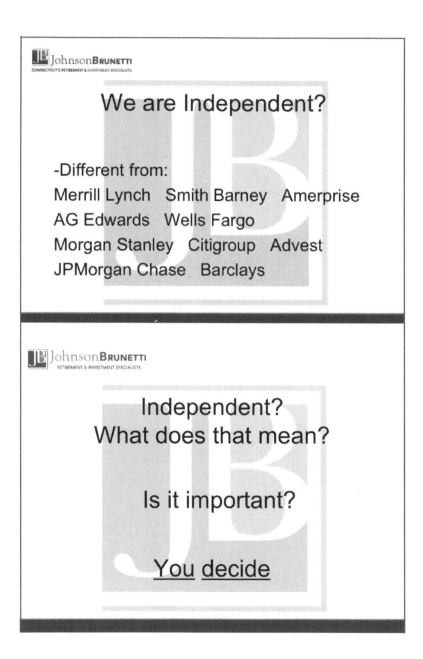

2. CHEMISTRY

The second important consideration is "chemistry." I feel it is important that you feel the person you're talking to understands you. If you are a husband and wife, make sure the person talks to both of you and also listens to both of you. If for one moment you feel that a broker is dismissing you or your feelings or is insulting or is coming across as arrogant, this is the wrong person to work with in my opinion. You may want to choose an advisor who understands you, who listens to you, and who will put together a financial plan that fits your needs and goals.

3. EMPATHY

Empathy. Does the advisor understand you and feel like you do when it comes to your important issues? You may have a special-needs child who requires special planning. You may come from a very poor family, one that lived through the depression, and you're worried about running out of money. Can that advisor relate? Does the advisor listen to and feel empathy for your particular fears? Another clue here that you may be working with the wrong advisor is he or she does not understand or does not listen.

4. ADEQUATE STAFFING

Staffing is a critical issue: it's where the rubber meets the road in today's financial world. Make sure the advisor you work with has plenty of service staff, and do so by simply asking. I know some firms where a broker handles hundreds of accounts without a full-time assistant, maybe sharing one with another broker. This isn't going to work very well. Two things can happen. Number one, the service level drops; number two, the broker or advisor has to constantly answer every phone call, every service inquiry. If I am talking to my advisor, I want one who is thinking about my investments, one who deals one-on-one with clients, not one bogged down by service inquiries and other issues that could be handled by a service assistant or a customer service representative.

Our firm has multiple advisors and an extraordinary team of both part-time and full-time professionals. Each advisor has multiple backup people. I think a good rule of thumb is at least a two-to-one ratio, two assistants per advisor in the firm. So a firm with two advisors should have at least four staff people backing them up. If you get lower than this in today's economy, when investment firms and insurance companies push more and more paperwork out to the financial firm than they used to do, for their advisors, it is going to be very hard for that broker to handle your account.

5. COMMUNITY RECOGNITION

It may be important to you that the broker or advisor you choose has a recognized name in the community. Let's think about a company like Disney. In Orlando, if somebody even writes the word *Disney* on a sign, Disney comes after them to take that word down. Disney makes sure that if it has the legal right to force the issue, it will do it simply because it wants to protect its reputation, a reputation second to none.

Other companies such as McDonalds and Coca Cola that have a very high level of service and brand recognition will do almost anything to protect that brand. They will decide not to take certain customers because they worry that those customers might be the complaining type, and the companies want to protect their reputation and their brand.

The same goes for financial advisors. Financial advisors who have a recognized name in a community will be very careful to bend over backward to do the right thing because they have spent years building their strong reputations and don't want to do anything to tarnish them.

6. AUTHOR = AUTHORITY

Is the advisor an author? Has yours written articles? Has yours authored books? Does he have any kind of ownership of publications out there, including a website? Is the website part of a big firm or is it independent?

Independent advisors will tend to have their own websites, not websites that are linked to big brokerage houses. It's helpful to know that your advisor has the expertise and the independence to write about subjects that are relevant to you. Being an author doesn't necessarily guarantee results, but it is something to consider. You can decide if that is important to you.

7. MEDIA PRESENCE

This goes along with number six—you may want to find an advisor who has a media presence. TV and radio stations typically have certain people they go to in the community who are able to speak on a number of different subjects. Has your advisor been on TV or the radio in the role of a local expert? This can be a good indication of a good reputation. Again, this is not the only factor. An advisor can pay for the time to get on radio or TV, so it's just another thing to keep in mind.

8. A GOOD BUSINESS PERSON

Does your advisor, or someone at the firm know how to run a business? This goes back to the difference between an independent advisor and one who is just an employee of the firm. How somebody can handle millions of dollars of other people's money and have no clue as to how to run a business is beyond me. It's also beyond me that somebody would choose to work with an advisor who has no employees, who has no banking relationship or even a business checkbook, and who does not spend his or her own money on marketing and reputation. This is my opinion, but the reality is that many financial advisors aren't in as good of financial shape as you may think they are.

You may want to find an advisor who understands the ins and outs of running a business, including hiring and firing employees, supervising customer service staff, and delegating issues as they come up instead of doing absolutely everything themselves.

9. GIVING TO THE COMMUNITY

Does the financial advisor give to his or her community? Are they willing to put money into the community, not just for the sake of publicity, but to have a meaningful impact. I'm talking about someone who is honestly trying to give to the world around them and to help when it comes to helping those in need.

10. CREDENTIALS

Does the advisor or people on their team have certain credentials. The CERTIFIED FINANCIAL PLANNER™ or CFP® is highly regarded in the financial advice world. CFP® professionals must complete extensive training and experience and are held to high ethical standards. The CFP® is awarded by The College for Financial Planning.

Other designations that are highly esteemed are ChFC® and CFA. The ChFC® is awarded by The American College and is usually awarded to people that have a life insurance agency background. It is a well respected credential that takes quite a bit of study to complete.

The CFA or Chartered Financial Analyst is very difficult to receive. It deals mostly with the analysis of securities, balance sheets, profit & loss statements and things that would be used by people managing money, but not giving advice to individuals like we do. Most Mutual Fund Managers are CFA's. If you are looking for one on one financial advice you would probably not seek out a CFA, but in my opinion, your advisor or their team should have a CFP® available at the firm.

Keep these considerations in mind when you are in the process of choosing a financial advisor. Try also to make your own list of your own values, as some on my list might not be important to you. But start with my list and begin to narrow down the advisors in your community; it is very possible that in an area like in an area like the Northeast U.S. that there are thousands of licensed investment advisors. You may come up with only 20 to choose from. Then you can begin to interview them, talking and listening, and end up with the one who is the best fit for you.

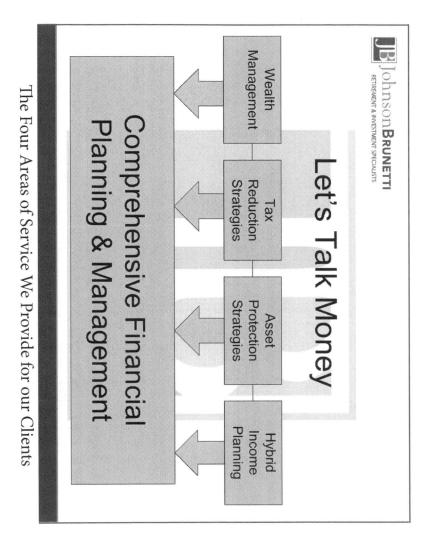

Let's Talk Money

Wealth Management

Tax Reduction Strategies

Asset Protection Strategies

Hybrid Income Planning

Comprehensive Financial Planning & Management

The Four Areas of Service We Provide for our Clients

WA

Made in the USA
Middletown, DE
26 April 2021